Beyond What We Can See

Beyond
What We Can See

The Afterlife and What Awaits Us

BEVERLY HOLLIDAY

DAGMAR
MIURA
LOS ANGELES

Published by Dagmar Miura
Los Angeles
www.dagmarmiura.com

Beyond What We Can See: The Afterlife and What Awaits Us

First published 2023

ISBN: 978-1-956744-94-1

Contents

Introduction .1
   How to Read This Book 3

What Happens When We Die? 5
Why Do We Have a Life Review? 13
What Happens When Children Cross Over? 21
Where Do Our Departed Pets Go? 25
What Does Heaven Look Like? 29
Who Is God? 37
What Do Angels Do? 39
What Are Spirit Guides? 43
Is There a Difference Between Spirits and Souls? 45
Do Animals, Insects, and Plants Have Souls? 47
Who Are We in the Afterlife? 49
What Is There to Do? 59
Are There Jobs? 71
Can Souls Have Romantic Relationships? 75
What Is a Soul Family and Who Are Our Soulmates? . . 79
Are There Holidays or Special Events? 81
What Other Creatures Will We See? 85

Do Our Loved Ones in Spirit Want to
    Communicate with Us?. 93
How Do Spirits Send Us Signs?. 95
Why Do Souls Want to Come into a Life on Earth? . . 99
How Can We Make the Most of Our Time Here? . . 103

Acknowledgments 105
About the Author. 107

This book is dedicated to Sam,
my greatest source of
comfort, inspiration, guidance, and joy.

Introduction

After more than two hundred conversations with departed relatives and friends, I've learned a multitude of fascinating details about the afterlife. So many, in fact, that the need to share them has become overwhelming.

This book is my attempt to answer questions about Heaven (aka "the other side" or "home") that many of us have likely pondered throughout our lives — and some that we might never have thought to ask. I acknowledge that I've learned only a minuscule amount about the afterlife and that some of my questions will not be answered while I'm still in the physical world.

How I became fortunate enough to have conversations with the other side came about following the passing of my daughter, Sam. Although I've heard tidbits of information directly from her, most of her messages have been conveyed through professional mediums. In the seven years since Sam departed, I've devoted much energy to communicating with her, as well as my father, and recording what has been divulged to me.

For those who are interested in exploring communication with the departed through the services of a medium, I'm offering my insight. Not all mediums (often called psychic mediums) possess the same gifts. Some only claim to be psychic and, sadly, are incapable of reaching the spirit world. Thankfully, I have encountered only one of these. However, in my search for talented professionals, I've been disappointed by several reputable mediums who simply didn't have the abilities I sought. I would like to acknowledge that most of these mediums do have gifts and seem genuine in their desire to help people — they just weren't the right fit with the spirits (especially my daughter) I was hoping to connect with. This can happen when a spirit doesn't feel comfortable with the energy of a medium and thus isn't forthcoming.

I've also learned that some spirits aren't good at communicating with humans, so this should never be held against a medium. Just as mediums possess different gifts and have varying levels of experience, so do spirits. Fortunately, Sam and my father (whom I will refer to as Dad from this point forward) are both gifted when it comes to verbal communication and imagery. Because of their abilities and eagerness to share, many of the descriptions of the afterlife in this book have been communicated by the two of them.

Sam frequently reminds me that many of the explanations that she, Dad, and other spirits have offered about the workings of the other side have been simplified, so that our human minds can comprehend them. In other words, don't be surprised when you first return to our heavenly home and find everything so much more extraordinary than what I've described!

One final point of clarification: Before you read some of the surprising details about the afterlife presented in this book, know that spirits can do whatever they want. Other people have written books about the afterlife claiming that spirits can't actually do physical activities, such as playing sports, creating art, or riding bicycles, because they don't possess concrete physical bodies.

Let me clear this up. If spirits want to experience physical activities on the other side, they can and they will. Throughout this book, I'll reveal many activities that Sam, Dad, other family members, and friends have enjoyed as spirits.

How to Read This Book

This book has been written to provide answers to questions about the afterlife in a sequential order. It begins at the moment a spirit leaves a person's body. From there, it will take you through the encounters, sights, and experiences that await all of us.

I recommend that you start at the beginning. You might be tempted to skip to certain topics, but I encourage you to refrain, because there are terms and descriptions in earlier chapters that will help you fully appreciate and understand the astonishing information that follows.

I hope you enjoy learning about the amazing life you'll live after you leave this one — just as I have.

What Happens When We Die?

M aybe the first question we should ask is "Do we actually die?" The answer is both yes and no. Only our physical body dies, and with it any physical suffering. But our spirit keeps on going. Some people describe this as our consciousness. It is our thoughts, emotions, and personality — our essence. As a matter of fact, some spirits don't even know they're dead (at first) because there doesn't seem to be a break in their thoughts. For example, someone who dies suddenly or unexpectedly might have to think for a moment to realize what has happened.

Whether they're aware that they're dead or not, some people are pulled toward a bright light, or pass through a tunnel, or both. These are common experiences we've read about, seen in movies, or have been taught. Although these can happen, not all crossings are the same. Some people are escorted by an angel or a guide and arrive on the other side immediately, and others enter Heaven in unique ways designed just for them. (Guides are departed spirits whose life experiences and training qualify them to offer direction.) The manner in which someone departs their body and crosses over depends on the type of death they had, the plans they made before their birth, and/or their needs.

Occasionally, a person's beliefs will affect their needs. Those who envisioned being greeted by a religious leader (such as Jesus, Muhammad, Abraham, Mother Mary, or the Buddha) might experience that. Someone who thought a tunnel was the only way to get to Heaven will probably travel through one. And those who expect to enter through magnificent gates (aka the Pearly Gates) will likely have that experience. However, the one belief about death that will never be realized is the experience of going to Hell. There is no Hell!

Heaven isn't just where we go when we leave our bodies. It's where we came from. It's our home, where numerous souls are waiting to reunite with us. Once the departed have reached the other side, they are usually greeted by loved ones who passed before them. This reunion is often followed by a welcome home event with many more souls, most of whom will be familiar from previous lives or will be extended family and friends the soul knew while on Earth.

The greeters will express their compassion for the challenges that were endured on Earth and will rejoice with the new arrival. The welcome home affair could be a very large celebration or a subdued gathering.

The following accounts were taken from interviews with family and friends who passed during my lifetime. Each story includes a description of both their passing and their arrival in Heaven. Although every arrival is unique to the individual, there's often some similarity in the experiences of those who passed in the same way.

Long-Term Illness

At the age of seventy-seven, Joe passed from heart failure due to Parkinson's disease. A man widely respected for his common-sense wisdom, he was known for communicating clearly — and as a spirit, he has demonstrated this same ability.

Joe described his passing in detail. First, he set up the scene. He said he was sick and weak, lying in a hospital bed at home. He did not need any assistance from a guide or angel when he left his body. Still in the room, he could see the family around his body and a guide near him.

He immediately thought, *This is better. Being out of the body is better.* Before leaving the physical world, he waved goodbye to everyone. At this point, he saw a white light and moved toward it. Although the guide was with him, Joe didn't need an escort to go into the light. He knew what to do.

Joe moved into the light and was transported through it, as if he were on an escalator that had no steps — smooth, like a ramp. He said the sensation was very peaceful and he felt warm, which seemed significant to him, because he had been feeling cold before he departed.

As Joe moved, he passed images and sounds of all the important and wonderful moments of his life — some of which he'd forgotten. (This wasn't his life review. That came later.)

At the end of this escalator experience, he was greeted by several family members and close friends who had departed before him. After this reunion, he stepped forward and was greeted by about a hundred more souls, who had come to welcome him home. This group was made up of other people from his life on Earth, as well as many he hadn't known in this lifetime. In an outdoor space, they formed a long receiving line to express their joy over his arrival. And to acknowledge an especially rewarding part of his life, there was a fire truck, which he recognized from his youth as a volunteer firefighter.

Unexpected Illness

Sam died suddenly, at the age of twenty-four, from acute pancreatitis. She didn't suffer for long; she explained that her illness wasn't severe, but it was her time to leave. As she left her body, she was aware of the presence of a guide and an angel. Even though she was a little confused, Sam said she couldn't experience fear; without a body, there was no racing heart, no shortness of breath, or any other symptoms of anxiety or panic. The guide explained to Sam what was happening while the angel provided comfort.

At first, there was darkness. Then Sam saw light and instantly found herself in it. She could then see all the guides and angels who had been with her throughout her life, but no one was communicating with her yet, because she needed to get oriented.

She found herself in a field of wildflowers. Barefoot, she walked for a few yards to get grounded. She said that she knew she had died and that she needed a short walk through the field to process it all.

After Sam's brief walk, others greeted her and welcomed her home. She proclaimed, "The amount of love is not even comparable to anything we can feel on Earth." There was a lot of activity, with a lot of spirits. And she teased that it was like Santa's workshop on Christmas Eve. Even though it was hectic, she had the ability to understand and hear everybody.

Because her life here was short, it didn't take Sam long to get reacclimated to the other side. To her, it seemed to happen quickly. However, time is very different on the other side. By the time her welcome-home activities were over, a couple of earthly weeks had passed.

Accident

Wilson, a vivacious twenty-five-year-old, saw his body lying on the ground after he was thrown from his motorcycle. In his determination not to end his time on Earth, he tried to reconnect with his body. He said his stubbornness prevented him from seeing the spirit guide who was there to escort him. Although guides have the ability and authority to tell a person that it's time to go, this guide didn't intervene. It had been preplanned that Wilson could linger for a few days — remain earthbound — if he chose. (An earthbound spirit is what people often refer to as a ghost.)

After watching and listening at his funeral service, he finally accepted his passing. It was then that he saw both a guide and his grandfather waiting for him. He knew it was time to go. At that moment, he also saw a bright light. He said it was like a camera flash. And immediately, he was on the other side.

Wilson instantly felt at peace, and although he was happy to be home, he still needed to get used to the idea that his life was over. He stood there for a moment, looking around and taking it all in, before interacting with the group of souls who had come to meet him. The gathering wasn't large and there was no party, as he needed to gently transition into the afterlife. Since Wilson had passed at a fairly young age, his parents were not yet deceased and

9

he recognized only a few souls from his recent life. Most were from previous-lifetime connections.

Dementia

During the last few years of his life, Mike's mental and physical health slowly declined as a result of dementia. When his body finally failed, at the age of eighty, his mind was no longer present in the physical world. He has no recollection of anything happening to him at the moment he departed. He now knows that he was taken to a place where he was comforted in a recovery chamber, until his mind was healed and he regained consciousness. This took the equivalent of about three earthly days.

The first thing he remembers was having the sensation of opening his eyes, as if he were waking up, and then hearing someone say, "You're back!" At this point, he moved to a space where souls had gathered to welcome him home. He was first greeted by friends and colleagues he had known in this last life. Next came his family and others with whom he'd had very close connections on Earth. He said these important reunions had been saved for last, as it would have been too overwhelming for him the other way around.

What happened next fit Mike's lifestyle and preferences perfectly. He showed images of the event. In a small but busy Italian restaurant, there were tables ladened with Mike's favorite dishes. He recognized all the souls sitting at the tables.

After acknowledging his arrival, everyone turned their attention to the food and began to eat. This welcome home dinner resembled countless family celebrations he had experienced throughout his life.

Suicide

Caldwell had lived a full and comfortable life. But when his wife — whom he referred to as "my bride" throughout their entire marriage — passed away, life became unbearable. At the age of eighty, he took his life, by gunshot.

This was not in his life's plan. However, he had committed suicide in his previous life, and his soul had wanted him to be tempted to do it again in this lifetime. (It's not unusual for us to put obstacles in our own way to learn a lesson.) Resisting suicide was an important challenge for Caldwell in this life, and it was a huge setback when he gave in to the temptation.

As soon as he left his body, he found himself in a thick fog. In reference to taking his own life again, he heard his main guide say, "Well, you're here again." Following this moment, Caldwell went straight into a partial life review. Before he was born into this last life, it had been planned that this assessment would take place immediately if he ended his life by his own hand.

As soon as this initial review was completed, the usual greetings began. His wife, Francis (one of his soulmates), was the first to meet him. Along with other family members from this recent life, he was soon reconnecting and rejoicing with other souls who were happy to see him. Just like Caldwell's personality, the celebration was a low-key event.

Murder

Annabelle was a single woman in her thirties who cared for and lived with her parents. Walking home in the dark after work, she was attacked by a man and strangled. She attempted to fight him off until she lost consciousness.

It was at this moment that she was taken from her body. (It's very common that a person's spirit will leave their body early if they're experiencing a traumatic death.)

She did not see a light or go through a tunnel. Instead, she instantly arrived on the other side. Annabelle wasn't a religious or spiritual person, and she was unsure of what was happening. She compared the disorientation to spending the night at someone else's home and waking in the middle of the night. It's confusing for a moment, and then you realize where you are.

In a space that looked like an empty white room, Annabelle was greeted by her grandfather from this past life. He explained what had happened, and she then remembered being strangled. She learned that her life had ended at the hands of a serial killer who'd been stalking her for about a month. At some point during their conversation, she recalled that her death by murder had been preplanned. Annabelle's quiet arrival was what she had needed. She said it was an "easing in."

Once she recovered from her tragic death, she found herself walking in a nature park with her grandfather. They talked about the life she'd just left. When they reached the other side of the park, they were met by all the souls who were waiting to welcome Annabelle home. There was no celebration. Anything festive at that time might have been too jarring for her.

Why Do We Have a
Life Review?

O nce we've reunited with loved ones and celebrated (or quietly accepted) our return to Heaven, we review all the important interactions and events of our lives and the related consequences we experienced and caused. The purpose of this review is to learn as much as possible from what we did and didn't do in our lives.

Higher Self

Before describing the life review, I need to introduce an important concept — the existence of a higher self. Not only do we all have one, but it designed us. It's our actual soul. While we're on Earth, it's on the other side, watching over us and feeling joy and empathy as we experience the highs and lows of our physical life. For us humans, this can be a difficult concept to grasp.

Before you were born, your soul — your higher self — made a comprehensive plan to send a part of itself into a life on Earth. Along with a council of its choosing, your soul decided what it wanted to learn and accomplish in this lifetime. In addition, it planned interactions with certain people who would be living at the same time as you. We are not only here to achieve the goals of our soul but also to help others achieve theirs.

These plans included the choices of who our parents would be. For some of us, they also included agreements with souls who would be our siblings, children, friends, associates, mentors, and romantic partners. Occasionally, souls agree to come into a life with someone who adds negativity (for example, an enemy). And sometimes, destinations are built into the plans — places that will assist us in learning our lessons. It's also possible that a feature of our arrival in Heaven has been planned. Take the Pearly Gates, for example. Not only are there people who have heard about them during their lifetime and expect to see them on their arrival, but there are also souls who specifically preplanned to enter through them.

The higher self makes many decisions during a pre-birth plan. But choosing the human's characteristics is of utmost importance. It takes bits and pieces from its collection of attributes — ones that would assist in attaining its goals — and then creates a human spirit.

Sometimes, a soul sends knowledge in a specific area, so that the person might demonstrate an unusual understanding of it. People who seem to have a knack for mechanics are a good example of this. Occasionally, a soul will include developed talents. This explains why there are people with extraordinary abilities that are apparent at a very early age — for instance, a musical prodigy. And sometimes, a soul will send a passion for a specific interest but not the talent. This revelation is wonderful news to me. Just because I can't sing in this life (at all) doesn't mean my soul is without the ability.

If you're like me, you might want to blame your higher self for choosing a life you had no part in planning. But wait. We're not off the hook yet. Before sending each of us to experience life as a human, our higher self requested our approval of the plan. So conceivably, we can take some responsibility for the decisions our souls made.

After arriving home and completing our life review, we merge with our higher self. We become one complete soul, acquiring all the knowledge, experience, and abilities that make up who we are in Heaven. Every soul has its own combination of gifts and attributes. And although many of these were developed through the experiences of our past lives, each of us will continue to add to our soul's collection of characteristics.

As I've been told several times, there are always exceptions to how things work in Heaven. There are cases where the higher self doesn't wait to merge with a person following their passing. When someone dies in a traumatic manner — such as by torture or murder — the soul sometimes merges immediately to alleviate distress and confusion. (It isn't until a person actually arrives in Heaven that negative emotions leave.) Then, when it's time for the life review, the higher self will separate temporarily, so as not to cloud the assessment of that lifetime (since the higher self has the memories and knowledge gained from similar challenges experienced in other lifetimes).

Sam illustrated what it's like to be a human, separate from the higher self, and then to reunite and become a complete soul. She suggested we imagine being in a horrible car accident and struggling through a yearlong recovery of learning to walk and talk again. Afterward, we would still be the same person but somewhat different, because we had this huge experience that changed us. So, in essence, our souls will be changed after each lifetime — and hopefully more evolved — but we'll still feel like ourselves.

A detail that I find especially intriguing and exciting is that before we merge with our soul (after our arrival), we can see, converse with, and even embrace our higher self.

Life Review

Certain aspects of all life reviews are the same. One of the most essential components is the review of the intentions that were planned before the life — the lessons that the soul wanted to work on. Then there's an assessment of how a person did in each category of these intentions.

A person's love life, family, career, education, and finances are examples of these categories. Each will provide opportunities to learn the lessons. Sometimes, a lesson can be learned in more than one area. It's also not uncommon for a soul to choose to focus on one or two categories more than others. For example, a soul could plan a life as a priest, with predetermined details in education and career but give little or no attention to romance. If no specifics are planned in a category, it's completely left up to the free will of the person.

If an intended lesson was learned, this would lead to spiritual growth. But if it was ignored, the soul wouldn't progress and could possibly descend — that is, move backward in spiritual development. A person can grow in one area but lose ground in another. And of course, there are people whose transgressions cause an overall, and more significant, setback in their spiritual growth.

During the life review, the newly arrived are comforted and supported by all the spirits who were present during their prebirth plan — their council. At the very least, this will consist of their higher self, their guardian angels, their main guide, and a few souls from their soul family. (A soul family is a group of souls who either have had many lives with each other or who have spent a lot of time together on the other side.)

Typically, it's the significant interactions and events that a soul will evaluate. Although a person can review everyday moments, this isn't common. Still, more than just highs and lows are looked at. There could be uneventful days in which a person had a sense that there was something they should be doing but ignored it. This too could be significant to the soul. Not every offense or missed opportunity is seen, but all of those relevant to the soul's journey will be included.

There's no grading on how a life was lived. No one is in trouble for what was neglected or the harm they caused themselves or others. Only understanding and compassion are expressed by the council. However, a major part of this educational experience is to feel empathy for others. This is accomplished by the person experiencing the hurtful emotions that resulted from what they said or did during their lifetime, as well as seeing the far-reaching impact of their actions. For example, if a father had bullied his son, in his life review he might see that the boy had tormented other children on the playground or had grown up to bully his own children. Perhaps a woman was berated by her boss at work and then went home and mistreated her family. This could be viewed in the life reviews of both the boss and the woman. Generally, the more harmful the negative action, the more lives are impacted. This ripple effect can extend very far.

During the review, souls will also get to see how others' words and deeds affected them. This is beneficial because they get to see the intentions of the other people. Someone might have meant to convey something very different from how it was perceived at the time. Often, we miss the true intent of what others say.

As much as some of us might wish that cruel people could feel the physical suffering they caused, this isn't what usually happens. The emotional pain is more important because it stays with the soul longer.

Although bodily harm is typically not felt during the review, a person can request to feel the pain they caused or inflicted on others in certain instances. For example, a soul who physically abused people might want to feel everything associated with their brutality.

If anyone reading this is concerned about how their misdeeds in this life will affect their afterlife, there's good news. Any resulting descension from the pain we caused or the lessons we missed can be worked on from the other side. For some, this may take a good while.

Perhaps you're wondering why souls are concerned about losing ground in their spiritual growth. Basically, it's the inherent goal of every soul to be spiritually fulfilled — to feel at peace with itself and to thrive as an integral part of the collective of Heaven. This is the most important mission of the soul.

The work that a person faces following the assessment of their life review doesn't begin until after merging with the higher self. Even though it was the human who lived the life, it was the higher self who originally planned the experience, with the hopes of learning and growing. Therefore, the ascension and descension happens on a soul level — the complete soul. Also, it's so much easier to see the true consequences and meanings of our actions once we have reunited with all the knowledge and experience of our higher self.

There are many ways that souls can evolve spiritually after descending. One obvious way is to experience (during the life review) the emotional pain they inflicted and reflect on it for a while. As mentioned, they can even request to feel the physical suffering. But again, it's the emotional trauma that affects us the most. Another way for souls to evolve is to incarnate into a life where they take on the role of their victims. For example, if a man abused his wife in one life, he could choose to be the abused spouse in his next life. Additionally, a soul can gain perspective and heal by becoming a guide to someone in the physical world who is facing the same issues.

Even though a higher self feels love and compassion for others, it can send a human spirit to Earth who possesses evil tendencies or compulsions. Molesters, murderers, and abusers of all kinds might very well have a higher self with exceptional qualities. Surprisingly, some of these horrible people come into a life with a prebirth plan to harm others. As an example, a higher self can plan for its human to be a serial killer. If the person does become a serial killer, there will be no decline in the soul's growth (regarding this specific part of their life) and many lessons will be learned from the experience — by the serial killer, the victims, and others associated with the murders.

What Happens When Children Cross Over?

S ince children have not been separated from the spirit world for very long, their departure from Earth and arrival in Heaven are usually more straightforward than those of adults. And when a soul sends itself into a life with plans of being sick and leaving young, the child will receive considerable comfort from the other side. Angels, guides, and/or other spirits will surround the sick child with a high-vibration energy (a positive energy that has been described as an "infusion of love"). Spirits will also send uplifting and soothing dreams to children who suffer. Some children are able to receive messages of comfort and guidance directly from angels or spirits because of their ability to see and communicate with them.

When children depart, their passings are smooth. There is no disorientation. They also feel more at home when they return, as they are much more connected to the spirit world than people who have lived long physical lives.

Seeing children on the other side isn't rare; however, it's not a common occurrence. When an infant or young child passes, they immediately merge with their higher self. There's no need for a life review. And when the spirit of an older child (usually older than seven) arrives in Heaven, it isn't long before it merges with its higher self. But before that, the older children will be able to reunite with their earthly family (if any passed during their lifetime) as well as other spirits they knew before their short life.

Adults who have severe mental disabilities will have the same passing and arrival as those of young children — they will immediately merge with their higher selves. However, those with a higher-functioning cognitive ability could have a brief life review before joining their soul. It all depends on the person's intellectual ability and self-awareness when they leave here. Interestingly, most of the lessons presented in the lives of people who have mental disabilities are planned for those who love them, take care of them, or are around them.

Although it's not a frequent occurrence for a soul to take on the appearance of a child in the afterlife, sometimes one might want to look like and play like a child. For this reason, playgrounds and other child-centered places can be seen on the other side from time to time.

If you are worried about missing the presence of children in the afterlife, know that you can visit Earth (or any planet) whenever you want. Perhaps you'll even be one of the spirits that's able to interact with them. Many of the imaginary friends that parents believe their children fabricate are actually spirits that only the young can see and communicate with.

Where Do Our Departed
Pets Go?

All animals return to Heaven when they leave the physical world. However, their arrival is much simpler than that of humans. When an animal spirit leaves its earthly body, it immediately appears on the other side, where it will reconnect with family and friends (animal and human) and express its freedom without any physical limitations or suffering.

Animals don't have higher selves, as we do. Their entire soul comes into their life and then returns to the other side upon their death. And they have no life review, as they don't have the complex intentions that humans have when coming into a life. There's no need to reflect on any pain or suffering caused or experienced during their lives on Earth. And since there's no need for them to contemplate physical challenges, animals are often taken from their bodies before they've completely died, to minimize their suffering.

Like human souls, animal souls only exist in a young form in Heaven when they want to. However, a fair number of animals enjoy being young, so they're easy to find when someone wants to hold or cuddle one. And if a human soul wants to spend some time with a young form of a particular animal soul, the animal can decide if it wants to do this.

Although animals can communicate with humans in the spirit world, the conversations are basic. There aren't any philosophical discussions. That said, I've had several conversations with pets who have crossed over and have discovered that they understand quite a bit. My most astonishing communication with an animal took place two days after my pet goat, Jelly, passed from a sudden illness at the age of six. He showed up jumping around, excited to talk to me. Aware that he had experienced a better quality of life than the typical goat, he expressed his love and gratitude to me. He also said he knew how much I loved him in this life. During our conversation, he told me he now has friends to play with and that one is his girlfriend.

Jelly revealed that it was in his soul's plan to live a short life. He came in with a predisposition to health issues, and he was ready to go when he got sick. He also said he would not return to this world until after I had passed, giving us some time to be together.

All animal souls have their own personalities. They also have preferences about which type of animal they want to be in the spirit world. Jelly prefers to be a dog. He's been a dog seventeen times on Earth. He agreed to come into this most recent life as a goat because I already had a pair of goats and it had been preplanned that he'd bring me comfort after Sam's passing. When my female goat got pregnant, it was the perfect opportunity for him to become my pet.

Although Jelly chooses to be a dog, he doesn't prefer a specific breed, so he frequently changes. He says his girlfriend also prefers to be a dog and likes to change breeds too. If they happen to be the same breed at the same time, it's purely coincidental, as they don't purposely coordinate.

Sometimes, souls ask the animals with whom they've had previous lives to come into another one with them. There are also souls whose love for animals is so strong that they want their favorite pets to hang around them in the afterlife on a consistent basis. But it's up to the animals to accept or decline these requests. If they do accept, the pets are free to come and go as they choose.

There are spirits working behind the scenes to match animals with people on Earth. Once they've found the right pet for someone, they coordinate an opportunity for the two to meet. Then they put thoughts like *This animal is supposed to be mine* into the mind of the person. Sam says those who find the matches are like elves and those who channel the ideas to the humans are like mall Santas — because there're so many of them. These same spirits also guide people to rescue animals in need. And on the rare occasion when an animal has saved a person, this also has been directed by spirits (think of the news stories about dogs who have dialed 911 to save their owners).

Wild Animals

Most animals on Earth are wild. A majority of these will return here over and over again. But they don't return immediately. Currently, only about 25 percent of all the animal souls are needed on the planet to balance the ecosystem. That leaves a phenomenal amount of them to relish life in the spirit world. When scheduled to return to Earth, animals can choose not to come. However, most don't mind coming back.

All animals have the ability to change their species in the spirit world. An animal that has never had a life as anything else might admire an animal of another type and choose to try it out.

What Does Heaven Look Like?

As a child, I imagined Heaven as a place where angels and deceased people floated around in the sky — far, far away, with God looming over everyone. And even though my imagination has evolved since then, it hasn't come close to capturing the descriptions that have been given to me.

Landscapes

In Heaven, spirits have a tremendous appreciation for nature. They can even create outdoor spaces themselves. However, not all spirits want to do this, and their levels of ability vary. Some of these places could resemble a favorite location on Earth, such as a stunning tropical beach or a crystal-clear lake near colorful mountains. Usually, these spaces are temporary and will either disappear when no longer wanted or will become something different. It's worth mentioning that spirits don't need to replicate an earthly location they enjoy because they can come here anytime they choose. We just can't see them. Well, most of us can't.

So what about the environments that already exist on the other side? The combination of features is endless. And some of the colors are truly out of this world, as there are so many more colors in Heaven than on Earth. Many places are considered permanent, because they've been around for a very long time. But in reality, they too can change. There are landscapes that look very similar to those on Earth and some that look a little like places here with added magical qualities. And of course, there are some that don't look anything like what we'd see on Earth.

The descriptions of nature, especially the beautiful landscapes, are something I expected, but I was astounded when I learned that there are also parks, resorts, and cities in the afterlife.

Parks

Every type of park that exists on Earth can be found on the other side. There are nature parks, city parks, theme parks, and even skate parks. Anything we can imagine and more exists in Heaven.

A city park might have benches, fountains, lampposts, paths, and lush grass — everything we'd see in a park on Earth. But a wonderful example of something that we don't have on Earth is a waterfall park, which is one of Sam's favorite places to visit. It has been in existence for a long time. She illustrated a beautiful, but unusual, scene.

It isn't like a man-made concrete water park. Instead, it consists of cascading waterfalls with pools between them. Each section is made up of different-colored water that slowly changes. At one moment, a waterfall could be pink fading into orange as the pool below turns from blue to purple.

Sam showed herself sliding down a waterfall in a bikini. Incredibly, when she began moving, most of the water stopped flowing and changed into a solid slide. She described the waterfall as "interactive" because the direction of the water's flow changes with each spirit, depending on their preference. One spirit might like a smooth, straight slide, while others might want curves or loops.

Although this park has short waterfalls ranging from five to twenty feet, there are other waterfall parks that have taller waterfalls of varying heights. Souls who want to prepare for a life that includes cliff diving will practice at the tall waterfalls (or at actual cliffs) in Heaven.

Resorts

Since anything we have on Earth can exist or be created on the other side, there are of course resorts. But why would spirits even need them? The answer is simple. Spirits have varying interests and desires, and they enjoy going to different places and experiencing new things. Just like us, they want a vacation or a break from their usual activities. Sam made the point — one that she has expressed several times — that it would be "lame" if spirits on the other side couldn't experience all the joys that human life offered.

For one of her heavenly vacations, Sam, along with a few other souls, went to a safari resort that had the look and feel of Africa. It's been around for a while. They rode around in jeeps and stayed in lodgings. Sam and one of her friends slept in a room that was built into the side of a hill. Dad, who was there at the same time, stayed in a cozy round hut. Lions, tigers, hippos, elephants, gazelles, and rhinos were just some of the animals they encountered on their excursions. There were even penguins. And if they wanted, spirits could interact with the animals. Since the need to defend or attack is absent on the other side — and there wouldn't be any physical pain if an animal got too rambunctious — anyone can touch the animals.

Ski lodges and tropical paradises are other types of resorts that have been mentioned. Dad particularly enjoys the island bungalows that sit over the water, like the ones you might see in Fiji or Tahiti.

Buildings

If there are cities, what's in the buildings? Surprisingly, many businesses are found on the other side. And many of them resemble those on Earth. There are offices, shops, restaurants, and community spaces, like learning centers and meeting halls.

Souls who were specialists in one or more of their lives sometimes want to share their knowledge and experience. It's not unusual to see offices occupied by physicians, attorneys, music instructors, art teachers, tutors, or those practicing any other profession that exists on Earth. These experts will offer advice or instruction to souls who are preparing for a future life or to guides who are helping a human with an issue.

If you love shopping and eating in your physical life, you'll most likely want to continue doing these activities in your afterlife. Fortunately, shops and restaurants can be found in almost every town or city. But who runs these places? Souls who enjoyed owning or working at stores and eateries when they were alive sometimes choose to provide the same services in the spirit world.

Salons and spas can also be found in the towns and cities. Certainly, a spirit can conjure up a hairdo or manicured nails without anyone's assistance, but for some, the physical experience and interactions with others make going to a salon more desirable.

At this point, you might be wondering how spirits pay for a service or an item. At first, the notion of stores in Heaven baffled me, but then I learned that bartering is the method of payment. The intent of the exchange is to show that you care about the other spirit — to express love. A good trade lies in the customer's knowledge of the other soul's interests. For example, buyers could give something they created. Or they could teach a lesson about something the person (clerk, server, or professional) is interested in. They could even offer a kitten or a puppy as payment. I find this last example humorous, because any spirit can cuddle an animal or acquire a pet whenever they want (if the animal is in agreement).

Although spirits don't need to read books to gather knowledge, there are libraries in Heaven. They have great value in the afterlife, as they are a tremendous resource for souls striving to continue their growth, as well as providing pleasure to those who love reading. One of Dad's favorite places to hang out is a gorgeous, ornate library that has several floors packed with books.

Museums can also be found in Heaven. Not surprisingly, there are many types. Some are similar to history museums. For example, there are buildings dedicated to each planet's evolvement. Even popular products or inventions can have museums dedicated to them — for instance, a coffee museum. And there are art galleries, many of which are interactive. When souls admire artwork in this type of gallery, they can smell the different objects depicted in the piece. A painting of cupcakes would smell just like cupcakes. Souls can also step into a scenic painting and experience being part of the landscape.

Basically, any type of structure that someone wants to visit either already exists or can be created in Heaven. And spirits don't just visit buildings with business establishments — they also spend time in their homes. That's right, spirits have homes. At first, I thought only the souls who had experienced life on Earth would want to have homes, but I was incorrect. Even though their dwellings can change periodically, as ours do, souls tend to have a permanent home base. And it's typical that only one soul resides in a space. Of course, souls can visit or stay over at each other's homes.

Sam has a townhouse. She said the exterior of the building was already there, but she created the interior space herself. At the time she shared this with me, she had mint-green plush carpet in it — something that she would never have chosen during this last life. Her place has a kitchen, a living area, a balcony, and a bedroom. Although they don't need sleep, there are souls who enjoy lounging in bed. I was reminded that relaxing in bed is a cherished activity for some people. Sam sometimes uses the bed for "checking out," which she describes as sleeping without dreaming. But she explained that if she wanted to, she could also experience dreams. Sam's place doesn't have a bathroom, as there is no need for one. Spirits certainly don't need to bathe, brush their teeth, or do anything that we associate with a bathroom.

Dad lives in a rustic and cozy cabin in the woods that he conceived himself. Interestingly, he periodically moves the woods. At times, he wants them only on one side of his home. Other times, he prefers to be surrounded by them. When he shared this, he lightheartedly added that there weren't many animals around his cabin because they didn't like the trees moving so often.

Buildings, just like landscapes, aren't considered permanent — even those that have been around for a long time. They can always change. When discussing the buildings and environments in Heaven, Sam playfully said, "We're not just up here floating around in the abyss."

Who Is God?

G od is the creator of everything everywhere. And because of this, he is often referred to as Source. He's also called other names, depending on the religion or culture.

We're all extensions of him, and his unconditional love for us is beyond our human comprehension. Since our souls are connected to him, we'll feel this same love toward each other in Heaven. And as spirits, we won't judge each other (only positive emotions can be felt and expressed).

God's powerful presence is felt throughout the spirit world. And although some humans are taught to fear him, this isn't an emotion they will feel once they arrive on the other side. Many people imagine such a formidable figure as a male. However, God embodies both masculine and feminine energy. (I use the masculine pronouns "he," "him," and "his" when referring to God only because those are the ones many of us are accustomed to hearing.)

If God is everywhere, can we talk to him one-on-one on the other side? Absolutely. But the experience might not be how we would imagine the experience to be. In Heaven, we can communicate directly with him telepathically. It's similar to when we silently pray here. However, in the spirit world, we will always hear his response. And when someone prefers, he will speak aloud — a different voice for each soul.

Souls can also have physical meetings with God, but this happens less frequently. Souls know when it's the right time to do this.

So, what does God look like when a soul is in his presence? Just like his voice, his appearance is different for each soul. It all depends on the individual's needs and preferences. For some, he might take the form of a man or a woman — as either a human or an alien. He could appear as a dog to someone who has a deep connection to animals. Others might meet him in nature, hearing his voice but not seeing him. And then there are some who prefer to see only his bright energy while they feel his presence and hear his voice.

Because Sam is a visual being, God portrays himself to her as an average-sized human man with brown hair and a curly beard. His clothes are white, and he is surrounded by a bright light. She says his voice is deep but soothing.

What Do Angels Do?

A ngels are unique creatures who have never incarnated into lives on any planet. Their primary missions are to protect, heal, and assist beings in their physical lives. They can come to our aid by their own initiative or respond to requests from us or our spirit guides. (Guides frequently need extra energy to protect us from extreme injury or death.) Angels also carry out acts of kindness. They can effortlessly manipulate earthly objects and will sometimes place our lost items in locations that are easy for us to find.

Various religions around the world (such as Christianity, Judaism, Hinduism, and Islam) have different classifications and names for the angelic realm. (Because of this, I have only mentioned terms and names that are generally well-known.)

Every person has one or two angels who accompany them from birth and remain until their death. These are called guardian angels. And it is typical for them to stay with the same person throughout many lives.

Even though people always have guardian angels with them, other angels will show up when needed. Along with the guardian angels, most of the other angels that come in and out of our lives are referred to as "working angels."

During emergencies, especially when preventing someone's life from ending too early, archangels are often the ones who swoop in to save us. They possess more abilities and authority than the working angels. There are many archangels delegated to each planet. Although most are responsible for only one planet, a few, like Archangel Michael and Archangel Raphael, will bring aid to other planets as well. Some archangels have specific areas they manage such as protection, healing, nature, relationships, love, hate, famine, and war. And each oversees hundreds of working angels, to assist in carrying out their responsibilities.

There are also angels whose authority is above that of the archangels. They are closer in proximity to God's energy and have been around the longest. The ones immediately next to Source have been here since the beginning. Their function is to relay information to and from the working angels and God. They are considered the "upper management" of Heaven and rarely interact directly with the beings on the planets.

In the afterlife, angels can appear as orbs, free-flowing energy, or tall physical beings with humanlike features. They can choose to have feminine or masculine energies, or both. However, they do not truly have gender. Archangel Michael is a great example of an angel who exudes tremendous masculine energy. Referred to as a warrior and protector, Michael has a large and powerful presence.

Angels also have the ability to look human when they are on Earth. They sometimes appear this way when they save someone's life or give aid in dire circumstances. In these situations, people occasionally think they're just Good Samaritans. Except when they appear as humans, there is a glow that emanates from angels, regardless of the form they take.

Whether angels truly have wings is a controversial topic. Fortunately, Sam has clarified this. They *do* have wings — considerably large ones. But they can choose not to show them. Although angels are rarely visible to or felt by humans, they sometimes wrap their wings around a person to offer comfort. They'll also do this to someone who has just passed from a tragic or abrupt death. In this situation, the departed will definitely feel the angel's healing love.

Each angel has a distinct personality. Some enjoy portraying themselves with masculine or feminine bodies and expressing themselves through apparel, hairstyles (long, short, curly, or bald), and color of hair, skin, and wings.

In Heaven, angels generally hang out with other angels. And even though they have the capacity to bestow tremendous amounts of love and affection, they don't have romantic connections. It's not uncommon for them to interact with souls other than angels, but they usually do this when they've been sought out. Angels are often called upon by others in the spirit world to share their knowledge, provide guidance, or assist in sending signs to loved ones in the physical world.

What Are Spirit Guides?

Spirit guides (or simply "guides") provide us support and direction. As previously mentioned, they've had experiences and training that qualify them to give guidance. Sometimes, they're that voice in our head that helps us make decisions — ones that will assist us in accomplishing our soul's plans. When our intuition says, *This seems like something that will be good for me*, or, *Maybe I shouldn't do this*, often it's our guides directing us. Also, like angels, guides can protect us in harmful situations. But unlike angels, guides are souls who have lived many lives and thus have acquired the wisdom that comes with considerable experience and knowledge of being human (or alien).

Our higher self chose one or two main guides to come in with us at birth and remain until we pass. It also chose other guides to assist us along the way. However, additional guides who weren't preselected could show up when needed.

Only a very small percentage of people will have two main guides. These people typically lead impactful lives. Jesus, Mother Teresa, and the Dalai Lama are a few examples. Those whose lives will involve extreme challenges, especially at a young age, will also have a second main guide.

Spirits who want to fill the role of main spirit guide receive special training. The other guides, who will assist us during different phases of our life, receive training specific to their area of support. If someone plans to have a child, a guide trained in infant caregiving could help them. Or if someone decides to start their own business, a guide with knowledge of business and finance might come to assist.

Interestingly, there is an exception to the required experience a spirit would need to become a guide. There are spirit guides who have never lived a human life. Although they've taken classes, they lack actual life experience. Some humans who come in with inexperienced main guides exhibit a preference for spending countless hours meditating and/or living simple lives, separate from society.

Is There a Difference Between Spirits and Souls?

Many people think the words *spirit* and *soul* are synonymous. Generally, they are interchangeable, but the biggest misunderstanding occurs when we compare a human spirit to a heavenly one. When we refer to living creatures on Earth, we say they *have* a spirit or soul. This is because they have a part of their higher self within them. But in Heaven, every being in the afterlife *is* a spirit or soul — with the exception of angels and God.

Here is where it gets a little more confusing. It has been conveyed to me that a soul is any creature that has the ability to be born into a life and return to Heaven. However, angels are souls, even though they don't incarnate. Interestingly, though, they are *not* considered spirits. Since angels are unique beings, they're referred to only as angels.

Do Animals, Insects, and Plants Have Souls?

As mentioned, animals return to the spirit world when they depart the Earth. Therefore, they have souls, regardless of whether the animal is wild or domesticated. They aren't as complex as human souls, though. However, in addition to instinct, animals possess certain intellectual capabilities and the ability to feel emotions, including empathy.

Insects also have souls, but they are far less evolved than animal souls. They feel hunger and some pain, as they have only a basic nervous system. They mostly operate by instinct, but they do experience fear. Since they have souls, insects exist on the other side. But let me assure you, they won't bother you in the afterlife. They don't need to defend themselves or harm anyone, and they stay in designated locations. If you don't want to see them, you can just avoid those areas.

Plants are different from other living creatures. They exist on Earth and in Heaven, but they do not cross over to the other side when they die. Therefore, they do not have souls. In the physical world, their energy is returned to the earth, to be recycled. In the spirit world, they exist because they have been created by God or any spirit who wants them around.

Who Are We in the Afterlife?

A s humans, we know that the specific combination of our characteristics — such as physical appearance, personality, abilities, and language — forms an individual different from anyone else on the planet. And even though there are many more souls on the other side, the same is true for them.

Appearance

Spirits in the afterlife can choose to take a physical form that resembles a human (or any other being that has incarnated into a life). And although their bodies aren't as dense as ours, they can change them to feel more solid whenever they choose. This would be beneficial when they're engaging in physical activities.

Riding a bike is an example of when spirits might want to feel solid. Yet, if there was a collision between two cyclists, their forms would change to be more transparent (a little cloudy, but you could see through them), and they would pass through each other. It's not something spirits need to focus on; it just happens automatically. This transformation is as natural as breathing is for humans. However, spirits could choose to remain more dense when they're playing a contact sport, such as football. They might want to feel the impact of getting hit or knocked down. Since there's no pain or injuries in Heaven, it only adds to the experience.

About 20 to 30 percent of spirits prefer not to look like physical beings. Most of these souls have never come into a life, and therefore, they've never had their identity associated with a physical appearance. These non-figured souls often present themselves in the form of orbs, which allows them to still be visible to other spirits.

Orbs glow with different intensities, and their light can be white or colored. Not only is there a huge range of colors to choose from, but also, the hues can have an iridescent quality. Although a soul can choose a color because it's partial to it, some colors are purposely used to provide identifying information. For example, the orb of a spirit preparing to come into a life will emanate a specific blue hue — one that doesn't exist here.

At times, souls will take the form of an orb when they travel to Earth, so they'll be more easily detected by animals (mostly mammals) and humans who have the ability to see spirits. Orbs are also visible in photographs. Interestingly, every soul can become an orb wherever they are, but not all souls have the ability to change into a physical form when they visit Earth (or any other planet).

The souls that want to look like humans or other beings in the afterlife will present themselves with whatever gender and physical features they choose. Many want to look the way they did in their late twenties or early thirties. Most souls who have lived many lives already have a collection of attributes that they favor, and they enjoy expressing themselves with a combination of these. Some souls, like Sam, change their looks often.

Curiously, the souls that have never incarnated any-where but choose to look like other beings won't neces-sarily possess the feminine or masculine energy reflected in their physical appearance. Any male or female quali-ties will come from their soul. In other words, if a soul who hasn't experienced any lifetimes on any planet wants to look like a beautiful woman but has male energy, the masculine characteristics will remain.

The small percentage of souls that choose not to have any physical appearance (not even as orbs) will remain as only energy. They can move about freely, but as Sam says, they don't "zip around" as much as orbs. This pure-energy state is invisible and nonphysical. It's used by all souls from time to time to reconnect with God.

There are various degrees of connecting with the energy of Source. When souls want to replenish their energy, they can choose a passive connection in which they have no thoughts or feelings. This is sometimes done before coming into a life or after returning from one. They can also choose to rest in a meditative state where they have some awareness and will still be able to feel the warmth of God's love. Other times, they might want to be in a more active state — for example, when souls have completed a lesson to their satisfaction and want to receive confirmation and acknowledgment of their evolvement. It can be similar to a graduation ceremony. And for some, an actual celebration follows.

Personality

As stated before, many of the characteristics we have possessed during our human lifetimes were planned by our souls. However, some of our personality traits were developed while we were here on Earth.

There could be attributes that our higher selves chose not to bring into this life, as well as those that they did. For example, Dad was considered a loner in this past life. He preferred to be surrounded by nature and live in a home isolated from neighbors. These preferences are a part of his higher self (a part of his soul's DNA). However, he was also socially awkward in this life, which contributed to his desire to spend a lot of time away from others. To my relief, he has acknowledged that the characteristic of being socially uneasy is definitely *not* a part of his soul.

The personalities of our complete souls are much more developed than they are here. They evolve through the experiences of all our lives and relationships.

Character

As humans, our moral nature reflects both the qualities of our soul and influences in our earthly life. Because we are sent here with free will and the ability to be influenced, our family and culture have a huge impact on our character. But on the other side, we possess the character cultivated by the experiences and knowledge attained through *all* our lifetimes and the continuous presence of love and acceptance.

Communication

Spirits converse in whatever language they prefer. Even though they might not know each other's words, they all understand each other. It could be said that there's a universal language of understanding. But there is no one specific language that everyone speaks.

Some souls occasionally want to talk out loud, but those that do still communicate through thought a good bit of the time. Sam enjoys talking aloud about 40 to 50 percent of the time, which is more than most. Just as human voices sound unique, so do those of spirits, even when they speak telepathically. However, not all communication via thought includes words. Any thought or intention can be transmitted.

If a spirit has never incarnated into a life, they can still learn languages. They might pick them up from others in their soul group, or they might choose to study them. Dad has acquired ten languages from past lives but has learned twenty-one from studying on the other side. He *really* enjoys learning languages — not just because of the pleasure he gets from studying them, but also because he wants to be prepared for future lives.

In addition to speaking, souls can sing. They all have the ability, but some are more gifted than others. And although they can sing telepathically, souls mostly sing aloud.

Interestingly, spirits can say things incorrectly — just as we do. On the other side, though, the intent of the message always accompanies the words. On Earth, we often can't be sure of the true intention of statements unless we know someone exceptionally well. A human could sound rude but not mean to, or someone could be speaking sarcastically while appearing to be polite. In the afterlife, there are no miscommunications.

Emotions

Often, I'm told that if something exists on Earth, it exists in Heaven. When it comes to emotions, however, this isn't true. Every positive emotion that humans possess can be felt and expressed on the other side. But negative emotions — such as fear, anger, hatred, sadness, jealousy, guilt, anxiety, disappointment, disgust, loneliness, boredom, frustration, embarrassment, rage, and apathy — don't exist once the life review has been completed.

That said, there's an exception. Souls who have never incarnated into a life might want to experience all the emotions that physical beings can feel. This is sometimes the case when a soul is preparing for a life. Fascinatingly, there's a special place that souls can visit to feel negative emotions, as well as other physical life experiences. It's been described as a virtual reality space.

Sense of Humor

At some point during my youth, I was taught that God has a sense of humor, and that's where ours came from. Today, I not only believe this, I know this to be true. I am constantly reminded that humor is undeniably present in Heaven. Sam, Dad, my guides, and even my higher self express their humor often. They claim spirits have an excellent sense of humor. They laugh too. A lot.

Pain and Discomfort

Just as negative emotions don't exist in the natural environment of Heaven, neither does pain or discomfort. However, as with emotions, there's an exception. Pain can be experienced by choice in a virtual reality experience.

As mentioned, during a life review, spirits might want to feel the physical harm they caused others. But there are other situations when souls could want to experience pain — for example, when a spirit is preparing for a life as a stunt person. Experiencing the pain that the human body would endure benefits their training. Fortunately, if something goes wrong, there are no actual injuries.

Taste and Smell

Spirits definitely have the ability to taste and smell. And they can choose *when* they want to use these senses, as well as *what* they want to taste and smell.

After being back home for a while, many spirits lose their desire to consume food. Because there's no physical sensation of hunger or the need to eat for survival, the heightened pleasure that we experience as humans no longer exists. Think about having an empty stomach and then taking that first bite of a freshly baked pizza or cookie. At that moment, the enjoyment is intensified. Since the sensation of being hungry and taking those first bites doesn't exist on the other side, the satisfaction of eating is different there than it is here.

Some of the souls who have never incarnated into a life have no desire for food. However, there are others who haven't experienced a physical life who occasionally want to try something that looks or smells appealing.

Sam's soul is a huge foodie. She also loved food in this past life. Something that has entertained me throughout the years since Sam's passing is her continuous love of chocolate. Numerous times, she's shown up eating a chocolate treat — cake, brownies, Oreos, chocolate-covered cherries, and even M&Ms.

When souls want to smell, it happens automatically. But the ability can be turned off when not desired. Spirits choose to enjoy the sense of smell most of the time.

Abilities

The abilities of a soul develop through eons of existence. They evolve through the soul's participation in the various activities of all its physical lifetimes, as well as its experiences on the other side.

Souls are drawn to certain things, just as we are. The reality, though, is that we (as humans) are drawn to an activity or interest because our higher self is. That said, we can live a life in which we're introduced to something that our higher self has never experienced. And this discovery can lead to a new passion and/or ability that will become part of our soul after we return home.

Satisfying Desires

When spirits look back on their human lives, they no longer have a connection with their earthly belongings, yet some spirits surround themselves with items that bring them pleasure. There's absolutely nothing wrong with having possessions in the spirit world. It's even acceptable to have every *thing* you want. This is not the same as having *everything*. Although souls can create any item they want, or do whatever they want, spiritual growth must be earned.

On Earth, you might feel guilty when others haven't acquired what you have. In Heaven, no one will be envious. Envy is not an emotion that exists there. Besides, all souls can have whatever they want. And you don't have to be concerned about earning or deserving what you acquire. Every soul deserves pleasure and fulfillment.

But how many souls really want possessions? Surprisingly, the answer is many. Some prefer to keep their afterlife simple and have only a few items, or nothing at all. Some surround themselves with a number of things they enjoy. And then there are some who go to the extreme.

A soul might choose to live a lavish life in a mansion with loads of stuff in order to prepare for an upcoming life of poverty. Because the subconscious will be accustomed to having everything, the person in that life will be challenged even further and will have the opportunity for more growth.

What Is There to Do?

I f we think of all the pastimes that bring people pleasure during their time here, we can get an idea of the
bare minimum of hobbies, interests, and amusement that
exist on the other side. Everything we can do on Earth
can also be experienced in Heaven — and much more.

Here are some of the activities my family and friends
have enjoyed in their afterlives: horseback riding, roller
skating, ice skating, soccer, racquetball, croquet, jet
skiing, water skiing, snow skiing, snowboarding, skeet
shooting, dancing, knitting, painting, hiking, bicycling,
sailing, yachting, sewing, going to theme parks, shopping, and eating.

Understanding how spirits do things physically

without a concrete body can be a challenge for the human mind. Here's what I've learned: Souls experience physical sensations. They can feel hot, cold, and touch. But again, they won't experience discomfort or pain. And when they're enjoying physical activities, they can feel the movements. Sam said she can even feel a breeze when she roller skates fast.

Another fascinating concept of the afterlife is how spirits manifest what they want. If souls want to go snow skiing, for example, they might use thought to arrive on a snow-covered mountain wearing skis and holding ski poles. Or they could have the skis and poles appear next to them and then put the skis on themselves.

Arts and Crafts

Sam is a gifted artist. In this past life, she was a digital artist studying animation when she passed. Her work is admired and appreciated by many in the spirit world. When Sam creates art, she uses different methods. Sometimes, she does it through thought combined with direction from her hands. She waves her hands to direct the paint (or any other medium). Other times, she uses her hands and tools (such as brushes and pencils) just the way humans do. Sam especially enjoys using her hands to make things.

She also likes to knit using only her hands, even though she says she isn't very good at it. Reflecting on lifetimes in which making clothes was needed for survival, Sam is currently attempting to improve her knitting skills for a future life. In one past life, she was surrounded by women who were adept at knitting. She admitted that she was not. Sam received friendly teasing for how imperfect her handiwork was, and she looks back on those memories fondly. She recalls when her kind and supportive husband in that life wore a sweater that she had knitted with one sleeve much longer than the other.

Interestingly, a spirit can make something by hand that has all the imperfections of something crafted by a human. Still, after making something this way, a spirit can manifest it into a perfect form, if desired.

Culinary Creations

Cooking is a good example of how spirits might choose to use their hands in conjunction with thought. As mentioned, some homes in Heaven have kitchens. This is just a personal preference. And a kitchen certainly isn't needed to have freshly prepared food. Anything can be conjured up anytime. And again, no one needs to eat in the afterlife.

Some souls, like Sam, not only love food but they also enjoy the act of cooking and baking. Sam has described how she baked a blueberry pie for Dad and herself. First, she went outdoors and picked the blueberries. Then, in her kitchen, she gathered all the other necessary ingredients using only thought. By hand, she made the dough and rolled it out to form the crust. After preparing the filling, she assembled the pie and baked it in her oven. When I asked her how it tasted, she replied, "Fantastic! Delicious!"

Games and Puzzles

Heavenly versions of hobbies can be much more involved and, for lack of a better word, *cooler* than they are here.

Take puzzles, for instance. One of Dad's favorite hobbies is putting jigsaw puzzles together. To emphasize the differences between earthly and heavenly puzzles, he described a gift he recently received.

It was a jigsaw puzzle of about 2,500 pieces, and it came in a box, as one would here. But instead of a scenic image on the front of the box, there were eight on the back. When a spirit starts the puzzle, the pieces correspond to only one of the pictures. However, the pieces change to correspond to one of the other scenes as the puzzle is being put together. Dad said he could be working on a scene of horses in the Wild West, and the next time he sat down, it might have changed to a picture of a bear in the woods. Depending on how long it takes to finish the puzzle, all the scenes could have rotated through. When the puzzle has been completed, the lines between the pieces disappear and the pictures continue to change — like a screen saver on a computer. If Dad wanted to take the puzzle apart and put it back in the box, or do it again, the lines would reappear and the pieces could be separated. He explained that *he* wouldn't be making the lines between the pieces visible again. It's a feature of the puzzle.

Another pastime of Dad's is playing games that challenge the mind. One of his regular games resembles our trivia contests. When he first shared this, I thought it was strange. Since souls can access knowledge they desire telepathically, it didn't seem like much of a competition. But Dad explained that while playing the game, contestants block their telepathic access to unlimited knowledge and use only their personal knowledge.

Gambling

Since all the games we have here are also over there, you might be wondering if spirits can gamble. They can, and some do. But no one goes home with any money. Every game or betting event is purely for entertainment.

Joe, who played poker in the physical world, still plays cards on the other side. He also has fun going to horse races. It's the excitement of strategizing and then winning that attracts him. He studies the statistics beforehand. When he gets to the track, he listens to the horses. Through telepathy, he learns their different moods. He also discovers if they're going to let a certain horse win that day. It sounds like cheating, but it's all for fun and nobody gets hurt. The horses aren't made to race. They choose to participate.

After Joe decides which horses he wants to place his bets on, he goes to the ticket window. Although he doesn't give the clerk anything, he receives a ticket for each bet. And just as people here will toss their losing tickets in the air, so do spirits. When Joe wins, he throws his ticket up and turns it into a miniature fireworks display. Another winner might toss a ticket into the air and it momentarily becomes a rainbow — or something else colorful or festive.

Cycling and Motoring

Riding bicycles and motorcycles are two of Wilson's favorite activities. He also gets pleasure from studying mechanical manuals and repairing vehicles. He has no current plans to come back into a life, but he says he might take his mechanical skills with him when he does. This hobby was something he enjoyed in his recent life. I remember watching him when he was a teenager having fun and getting satisfaction from reading a manual and then repairing his old Volkswagen van.

Some spirits get tremendous pleasure from driving cars. Scott, who passed unexpectedly at the age of thirty-nine, has expressed that he feels an immense sense of freedom when driving fast on the other side.

Entertainment

By now you might suspect that every form of entertainment we can think of will either be found or can be created in Heaven. And this is true — with the exception of anything that causes harm. Video games? Yep. Sporting events? Of course. Newspapers and magazines? Absolutely. Car races? You bet.

For spirits who are drawn to creating theatrical productions and musical performances, the same roles required on Earth are needed: playwrights, composers, musicians, actors, vocalists, dancers, set designers, directors, and so on. Many of these spirits take on these roles because of their love of music or theatrical arts, but they don't always do them for their own enjoyment or to entertain an audience. Some souls might be working on a skill set that will benefit them in a future life. Along these same lines, a soul planning on being a spirit guide might want to brush up on the skills their human will need.

Since movies are a big part of our entertainment here on Earth — and so many of us love them — we can certainly count on them to be in Heaven. But they don't just exist there; that's where they originated. All the innovative ideas of humans have been inspired to some degree by souls on the other side.

Sam adores watching movies. She especially enjoys going to cinemas with a group of friends. They eat popcorn and whatever else they want. Sometimes, she goes to movie theaters that serve meals at tables. She says any of the theaters could be made to look and smell like ours on Earth. Teasing, Sam revealed that the floors could be sticky if she wanted to capture the whole human experience.

Some souls have TVs in their homes and have been watching them long before humans had them. In Sam's living room, she has both a TV and a couch for viewing. The display appears on the wall without any equipment. Sam admits that she likes watching movies at home even more than going to the theater. To make a selection, she either brings up a show or movie by thought, or she does it the same tedious way we do — by scrolling through a long list of choices. Interestingly, there are souls who do the programming for the TVs. Many do this because they want to learn about the workings of appliances and/or technology (again, for a future life).

Occasionally, Dad and a few friends join Sam for movie nights at her place. They gather in the living area, where there's a sectional couch and a large square ottoman for everyone to put their feet on. And just like we do, they munch on popcorn and other goodies. But here's where it gets truly fascinating. Sometimes when they watch a movie, they participate in it. Sam asserted, "Movie night over here is an immersive experience!" She showed images of the group white-water rafting in one movie. And in another image, she appeared inside a Tarzan film wearing a short dress (resembling an outfit Jane would wear) and swinging through the jungle with monkeys. Sam also revealed that she will alter the end of a movie whenever she wants to change things up or she doesn't like the original ending.

The viewing of a show or film can take place anywhere. Sam perfectly illustrated this. She said you can be on a raft in the middle of the ocean and watch a movie. After all, why not?

Fishing and Hunting

Believe it or not, spirits can even fish in Heaven. However, instead of hooking the fish or trapping it in a net, the experience focuses on expressing appreciation through a harmless "catch and release." And because some spirits still desire the thrill of tracking animals, the sport of hunting also exists on the other side. Although no animal is hurt in any way, there are spirits that want to relive the activities associated with hunting. These could include a hunter searching in the woods while trying not to make a sound or sitting outside for long periods in a duck blind or deer stand. The objective would be to locate and then show admiration for the animal. The steps a spirit might take to enjoy fishing or hunting truly depend on the individual.

When Sam goes fishing, she puts a glowing light on the end of her fishing line (instead of a hook). From a shoreline, she casts out into the water. When a fish sees the glow, it has the option to accept the invitation and play along. If the fish is interested, it will put its mouth around the end of the line, and Sam will reel it in. Once it has reached the shore, the fish and Sam acknowledge each other. She said this is mostly done through eye contact. Then Sam expresses her appreciation and puts the fish back in the water.

Camping

Since there are many people who love spending time outdoors, it's no surprise that there are some who enjoy camping on the other side. Seven years after her passing, Sam shared a new adventure with me — one that I consider to be the perfect camping experience. Using her imagination and artistic abilities, she created a huge treehouse complex for spirits seeking amusement in a camp-like setting.

At the top of tall trees, this whimsical creation was built in a place that already exists. The surroundings resemble Hawaii, with mountains and beautiful waterfalls. There's also a river that's ideal for kayaking or tubing, a quarry hole for swimming, and caves for exploring. And the water in each area is clear yet has an intense blue color.

This heavenly camp offers many opportunities for souls to entertain themselves. Among the activities that were initially planned (in addition to kayaking, tubing, swimming, and exploring), spirits can ride bicycles, hike trails, or play horseshoes. There are even scheduled movies. Sam flashed an image of someone floating on the river in a tube while watching a movie on a big screen — located on the shore so that many could watch.

Just like everything on the other side, whatever you want to do at this camp, you can. Dad enjoys riding around in a golf cart and birdwatching, as there's a wide array of birds in this place. Sam showed herself shooting at targets with a bow and arrow. Of course, there are campfires, where souls gather for social activities like playing instruments (guitars, ukuleles, and drums), singing, roasting marshmallows, and making s'mores.

To make campfire activities and other nighttime

entertainment more pleasurable, the area has a night cycle. Sam explained that God created some areas in the spirit world with this feature because there are souls that like the change. Those who have experienced many lives on planets have become accustomed to alternating between day and night. Many still enjoy activities that are more spectacular in the dark, such as campfires and fireworks. But anyone who doesn't prefer the darkness can pop someplace else until daylight appears. (It should be noted that any soul can make the space around them dark or light whenever they choose, but they cannot create an automatic rotation of day and night.)

Although Sam was the original designer and creator, others have added their own treehouses to the camp. Sam's home, along with several others, is in the shape of a ball and has the appearance of wood. Some souls, however, have created more traditional spaces. There are open-air treehouses with only a roof, as well as some that are enclosed and have windows. At the time I learned about the treehouses — soon after Sam began the community — there were at least fifty of them.

Around the camp and placed low to the ground are hammocks. High above, ropes hang down for swinging from area to area (like Tarzan). One rope is set up for swinging over the quarry hole and jumping into the water.

Between the treehouses are rope bridges. Most of the bridges and houses have the look of natural rope and wood. However, some have been painted colors to suit individual tastes.

Surprisingly, Sam's ball-shaped house doesn't look round inside and feels much larger than it appears from the outside. It has windows that she can close when needed. When Sam shared this, I was a bit confused.

When would someone need to shut out anything in Heaven?

She explained that she occasionally wants to tune out the sounds of others and feel cocooned in her own space. Apparently, it can get loud when so many are enjoying themselves, especially if there's music and singing. Although souls can block sound any time they want, Sam prefers to do certain tasks with her hands, such as shutting a window. She said she likes the feeling of performing actions that she was accustomed to doing in her physical lives. For example, when she opens a window, it reminds her of when she was alive and opened a window to let in fresh air. It brings a sense of ritual and pleasure.

Although the camp environment lends itself to more rustic dwellings, Sam has added features to her treehouse that might seem a little excessive for camping. But again, the afterlife is about satisfying your interests and desires. In her space, she reads, watches TV, and relaxes in her hot tub. In a large open space there's a living area, a kitchen, a bed, and sliding doors that lead onto a balcony.

This isn't just a getaway for Sam. She and some others have decided to reside in this camping paradise for a good while.

Are There Jobs?

In the afterlife, souls work on lessons and missions, but they don't really have jobs they *have to* perform. If they choose, they can seek out guidance for a project or endeavor, but no one tells them what to do. It's ultimately up to each spirit to decide what they want to work on or explore. Some might spend energy learning a trade or taking classes to prepare for a future life, while others might focus on unfinished lessons from their most recent life. Some could channel inspiration or support to those incarnated in a life. And still others could provide a service to the spirit world. Any soul could do all or none of these.

Some choose not to do any type of job for long periods of time. This often occurs after completing a life. Relaxing, having fun, and reconnecting with others are the activities that most souls focus their attention on when they first return home.

Spirits that want to learn something new (or expand their knowledge or skills in an area) can take classes, read books, watch instructional videos, seek out knowledge from someone with expertise, or get on-the-job training. It is possible to master skills or become an expert in a field without ever experiencing it in a physical life. For souls who want to access information without investing energy, they can simply tap into records telepathically. But this isn't typical when the goal is to learn a skill or trade.

In addition to providing us with inspiration, spirits offer other types of assistance to humans. Sending us emotional support is one way they help. This is a top priority of our loved ones. Some become spirit guides, though this is undoubtedly a major commitment, especially for a main spirit guide. And, unfortunately, we don't always pay attention to the guidance they offer us.

Souls will also help people with whom they have no connection. Many spirits, including Sam, offer aid and encouragement to those who help the less fortunate on Earth. Sam is especially focused on bringing relief and comfort to children. She also sends enlightenment to people who will spread it. There is a particular teenager to whom Sam, along with a group of other souls, is sending inspiration. As an adult, this girl will have a huge influence spiritually on the world, whether it's through books, movies, or other media.

A soul who is gifted in a particular area might also choose to send ideas to a person with the same talent. Sam does this off and on. She has a passion for inspiring people who are writing fictional books and screenplays.

Sam revels in the ability to change her goals on a whim, as her interests are very diverse. A few months ago, she mentioned working with a group of spirits on a project developing technology for water therapy on Earth. The intent is to bring healing to those with mobility issues and children with severe autism. This invention will eventually be sent as a vision to somebody on Earth.

Since his passing four years ago, Dad has shared two service-related functions he performs. As a sidenote, it was a full earthly year before he started either of these. This emphasizes the point that souls work when they want to — or when they are ready to.

One of Dad's jobs is to train service animals, especially dogs and horses, who will return to Earth with the plan of assisting people or providing therapy. Although the animals won't have a conscious memory of their training once they are here, they will instinctively follow commands and learn more quickly. Working with animals is a mission Dad had before coming into his recent life. Although his connection with animals was blocked from him while he was here, his soul has enormous love for them. Some of the animals he trains could end up being entertainers — or, at the very least, wonderful pets.

And recently, Dad has picked up an important task that serves the whole collective of the spirit world: he's updating records by cataloging books and artifacts. This is another area for which Dad has considerable passion. In addition, he's channeling information related to this undertaking to a museum curator here.

Jean, who was a nurse, mother, and community activist in this past life, sends help to pig farmers on Earth. It's not that this is a major mission of hers. She just loves pigs. And they love her. She spends a good bit of time with them on the other side, especially her cherished pigs from a life as a farmer in England. Utilizing her medical knowledge from previous lives, she nudges farmers to check on their pigs when she sees something is wrong.

Being a barista, architect, chef, teacher, hair stylist, event planner, and mentor are other examples of how spirits can be of service in Heaven. The types of jobs that give a soul purpose in the afterlife are endless.

There are also large-scale projects carried out by souls.

During the first year of the COVID-19 pandemic, a multitude of spirits worked in numerous roles to provide the whole world with emotional support, as well as to provide inspiration to the scientists developing vaccines.

Can Souls Have Romantic Relationships?

Many people want to know if they'll be able to reconnect romantically with their partners in the afterlife. For those concerned, it's absolutely possible. If two souls feel romantic toward one another after returning home, they can certainly have a romantic relationship. It might be long-lasting, but it also could be brief or intermittent. Souls can reconnect with each other even if their intimate connections took place centuries ago.

Not only does romance exist in Heaven — the equivalent of sex does also. However, there's no sexual interaction physically between spirits. Even when souls take on a physical appearance (like that of humans), the anatomical parts for sex are nonfunctioning. So, although spirits can have physical sensations when they touch something — like kicking a ball or feeling a cool breeze — they don't have the sensations caused by hormones or any physiological system in the human body. Two souls can put their lips together in a kiss and feel the sensation of touch, but they won't feel the same warmth, pleasure, and desire that humans feel. Imagine placing your lips on those of someone for whom you have no feelings. You would feel their lips against yours, but there would be no arousing sensations.

So how do souls "do it"? When they want to express their romantic affection for each other, they simply merge their energies. It is through this exchange that the chemistry is felt. They will stay connected until they have received the amount of pleasure they desire. In other words, if souls want to express the gentle affection that is equal to a quick human kiss, the exchange of energy would be brief. And if souls want to more fully express their love for each other, they could remain together until the intensity is similar to what humans experience during sex — or greater. Sam has insisted that the sensations of sex on Earth don't compare to the euphoria that can be experienced during an intimate exchange of energy in Heaven.

Remarkably, when souls take on the physical appearance of a human, most of them choose to have all the parts — even those that don't work. It's what many souls who have incarnated on Earth are accustomed to. But again, there's no arousing sensation associated with any physical features.

Animals can also express intimate love on the other side, and they also do this by combining their energies. And since there isn't a risk of producing offspring, the union of different species isn't a concern.

Interestingly, the afterlife doesn't have any rules or social values about monogamy. A soul could merge energies with one soul frequently and still have exchanges with others. And because so many delight in expressing their romantic connections, even weddings are a common occurrence on the other side. However, a ceremony is basically held for the fun of celebrating a couple's love. The souls aren't tied to each other in any way other than by their love.

What Is a Soul Family and Who Are Our Soulmates?

A soul family consists of a group of spirits who have gravitated toward each other over time. Generally, they're made up of souls who have had a lot of lives together and have become very close. The number in each family varies. A large group would have thousands whereas a small group would have two or three hundred.

The groups are constantly changing and growing. There are no restrictions; spirits can come in and out of soul families, and some can be in more than one at the same time.

Spirits who enjoy being together and who have forged a strong bond are called soulmates. Their connection takes a long time to develop and is usually achieved by experiencing many lives together. And the relationships aren't just romantic, as many people believe. Sam is one of my soulmates. We have experienced more than 150 lives together.

Throughout the many lives that two souls spend together, whether they are soulmates or not, they change up the nature of the relationship. For example, Sam and I have been mother and daughter, father and son, sisters, brothers, friends, acquaintances, and so on. This has given us the opportunity to experience more and, therefore, evolve more. In the spirit world, our relationship is similar to that of best friends or close sisters.

All soulmates are in the same soul family, but they don't always start out that way. Since souls can be in more than one group, they can join the families of their soulmates. Everyone has multiple soulmates — some even have dozens. Souls that incarnate often generally have three to five that are considered more significant than the others. It's typical to bring only one or none into a lifetime. Very few souls choose to have more than one soulmate accompany them when they incarnate.

Are There Holidays or Special Events?

S ouls who enjoyed certain holidays when they were alive tend to continue some of the same customs. Although birthdays don't hold much sentimentality once a life is over, popular holidays, like Christmas, are celebrated by many in Heaven.

While watching their loved ones celebrate special events on Earth, spirits will often participate in similar festivities. This is a way for them to feel connected to us. They also send down energy to anyone who's struggling during these emotionally intense times. (Every living thing has a vibration, and spirits have the ability to adjust ours to allow physical or emotional healing.)

Although Sam makes a point every year to assure me

that she's with me at Christmas, she thoroughly enjoys partaking in her own holiday traditions. She watches holiday movies and decorates her home. She says there's a lot of joy in putting out the ornaments and trimmings herself. Later, when she wants to take down the decorations, she simply focuses on their removal and immediately they're gone.

One Christmas, Sam and Dad attended a gathering of about thirty to forty spirits. It was held in a ski resort lodge. A dinner was catered, and presents were exchanged. Similar to a "Secret Santa" event, each soul brought one gift for someone else. It was at this event that Dad received his eight-image interchanging puzzle (mentioned earlier). The spirit who gave him the present knows how much Dad loves puzzles. Sam received a unique and beautiful candle in a handcrafted metal stand. It was made by the soul who gave her the gift — an artist learning metalwork.

Not every spirit that delights in Christmas (or other religious) rituals has had a life experiencing them. It isn't uncommon for souls to want to join in the fun or try something new.

Heavenly Events

There are also celebrations that exist only in the afterlife. Several are huge and include any soul who wants to participate. Sam attended one that was so magnificent, she couldn't wait to tell me about it. There were copious amounts of food, music, and dancing. The event was divided into areas that represented the vast cultures of our earthly countries, as well as those of other planets. Many dressed in the attire that corresponded to each area they chose to attend.

As one of their many experiences at the event, Sam and Dad joined in the German festivities. Sam showed them dancing together. Dad wore lederhosen and Sam wore a coordinating woman's outfit — a dress with a white apron and hat. Three of my guides shared some of the costumes they wore at the individual parties: Viking, Scottish, Irish, and American Cowboy. In one of the areas, a guide changed his appearance to that of a creature from another planet. He looked humanlike but taller, with elongated features.

The celebration was a great opportunity for souls that hadn't experienced many cultures (or had never incarnated at all) to try various types of music and food. Some had never tasted food before.

Even though all the areas were in the same place, the music was contained within each one, as if magic soundproofing had been placed between the sections.

This colossal event lasted more than a week in earthly terms. Large-scale celebrations like this occur only every decade or two (in earthly time). However, smaller ones take place on a regular basis.

What Other Creatures Will We See?

Of all the amazing details that have been divulged to me from the other side, some of the most surprising are about the various spirits that exist there. If we consider all the types of people and animals that have lived on Earth, including dinosaurs, we can imagine only some of the creatures that we'll encounter in the afterlife. As previously revealed, souls that have incarnated on other planets are as much a part of Heaven as earthly spirits are. And it's possible that your soul has sent a part of itself into a life on another planet — maybe lots of lives on several planets.

If that doesn't surprise you, this might. There are creatures in the spirit world that we on Earth believe exist only in fairy tales. Of course, there are some characters in our folklore and stories that are mythological — they don't exist anywhere. But those that do, exist in physical lives on other planets or solely in the spirit world. These include Bigfoot, the Loch Ness Monster, mermaids, fairies, and unicorns. Bigfoot and fairies visit our planet often. The Loch Ness Monster and mermaids come here infrequently. And unicorns have never visited here.

I'll admit that the concept of mermaids, fairies, and unicorns existing is unfathomable at first. But I've heard about these mystical creatures repeatedly over the past few years, so for me it's become easier to grasp. Here's my logic: if I can acknowledge that there are angels — with their magical qualities of being invisible and having wings — why can't I believe that God created other mystical beings?

Bigfoot and Yeti

Have you ever wondered why so many people have spotted the apelike creatures we call Bigfoot and Yeti but no one has been able to get close to them? Well, there's a good reason for this. Bigfoot (also known as Sasquatch) and Yeti possess the ability to become invisible. They're also able to exit our world in a split second — if they're in the right location. To leave Earth, they must be in the energy field of a nearby portal. Located around the globe, portals are openings to pathways to and from planets. They can be thought of like a bus line, or a subway system, that comes from a faraway place and branches off to different locations. Portals are the only way Bigfoot and Yeti can arrive here.

These two types of beings visit our planet because they like our remote forests and mountains, where animals, fish, and fresh water are available. This is why they're often spotted near rivers and lakes. They have respect for nature and try not to leave behind any evidence of their dwelling.

They might look like apes, but they're more evolved. Apes here are primarily vegetarians; Bigfoot and Yeti are carnivores. Their level of intelligence is closer to that of our higher-thinking animals, such as whales, dolphins, and elephants.

Bigfoot has been spotted in North America, and Yeti has been seen mostly in the Himalayas. They belong to the same species, but they have their differences. Bigfoot is the least aggressive of the two. Neither breed has the desire to interact with humans, and whenever they believe they're at risk of being harmed, or if they don't want to be seen, they exit or temporarily become invisible.

Their home is on a planet in another solar system. Other beings that belong to this species live there but have not felt the need to come to Earth. In their world, the Bigfoot and Yeti species is close to the top of the hierarchy of inhabitants. However, these beings have an animal energy. Therefore, any animal soul can choose to incarnate as one of them.

Bigfoot and Yeti have the ability to communicate telepathically as well as verbally. And although human spirits can speak with them in the afterlife, the two groups don't hang out together.

Mermaids

Mermaids (and mermen) do exist, but their appearance isn't as glamorous or as colorful as they're portrayed in our fairy tales. And although they used to stay for extended periods of time on Earth, they no longer inhabit our world. Though that's not to say they haven't visited recently. But a sighting is rare, because their visits have become infrequent. Just as Bigfoot comes here through portals, so do these extraordinary creatures. (Portals are located in oceans and lakes as well as on land.)

Mermaids are from a planet in a faraway solar system. Their world is almost completely aquatic. There is some land, but all creatures there live in the water. Mermaids can swim up to the coastline and lounge for a while, as they can breathe both out of water and underwater. Living a life on this planet has little to do with evolving, as a human life does. There is no complex thinking — nothing to intellectualize, no problems to solve. The whole purpose of life there is to experience having a physical body.

Mermaids have something similar to hair on their heads. It grows very slowly and never needs to be cut. Their faces do not resemble ours. They have breasts, arms, and hands, as we do. Their hands are designed for swimming, though, with webbing between their fingers. And just as we've fantasized, they have tails covered with scales. To communicate, they converse either telepathically or verbally. Their vocal sounds resemble those that dolphins make.

On the other side, mermaids are found in the water or lounging next to it. Created only as water creatures, mermaid souls are very different from ours, and human souls cannot incarnate as them. However, if, during the afterlife, we ever have the desire to experience the life of a mermaid or a merman, we can change our form to theirs and temporarily inhabit their planet.

Interestingly, most mermaid encounters on Earth are orchestrated by spirits from the other side. These events are more about humans experiencing the "unexplained." They lead us to know that the universe is much more than we can imagine.

Lake Monsters

Popular myths about lake creatures also hold some truth. The most famous example is Nessie, from Loch Ness in the Scottish Highlands. Although it does exist, it spends most of its time on its own planet. This creature is from a breed that is friendly and sociable with the advanced beings in its world. It is considered to have a gentleness similar to that of our manatees.

One of the reasons that Nessie chose to temporarily inhabit Loch Ness is because there's a portal there. The creatures of this breed can also inhabit our oceans, as they thrive in saltwater as well as freshwater. But a sighting in the ocean is much more unlikely, since the ocean is so vast.

Fairies

Popular figures in folklore, fairies have captivated people for centuries, especially in Ireland and parts of the United Kingdom. They are still part of the culture in Ireland, and constructing fairy gardens is a common practice there. But these gardens are more than ornamentation — because fairies truly enjoy visiting them. And these quirky creatures prefer the gardens that have been constructed by the humans who believe in them. When they choose to inhabit our planet for lengthy periods of time, they settle in all-natural environments away from human activity.

Fairies are like angels in the sense that they were

created to remain as spirits with specific purposes. They cannot incarnate into a life. Therefore, they are not from another planet, where they would require food and shelter. And although they have no physical needs, they occasionally consume plant treats, like berries and the nectar from flowers.

We cannot incarnate as one of them. But just as with mermaids, human spirits can create and temporarily take on the body of a fairy, if there's a desire to experience what it's like to be one.

On the other side, fairies are a little shorter than half the height of an average human soul. And like angels, they have wings but can choose not to show them. When they visit Earth, they are very small — no larger than a hummingbird — and can become even smaller when they want.

Even though fairies can visit Earth in their natural spirit form, they usually appear in a concrete physical form, allowing themselves to have the whole experience of living in nature here. They enjoy interacting with animals, frolicking in and around plants, and feeling the elements. Rain irritates them, but interestingly, they don't mind the cold (unless it's freezing cold). They prefer to be invisible around humans. And although it's extremely rare, people have seen them.

They have lean figures, and their hands and feet appear elongated compared to those of humans. As spirits, fairies don't need clothes, but they usually wear them. When on Earth, they dress for the weather. In winter, this could include jackets, hats, boots, scarves, mittens, pants, and leg warmers. Fairies have an affinity for fun and colorful clothes. Not only are their clothes colorful, but their skin and hair can also be various hues — pink, blue, green, yellow, or whatever they want. They also have colorful auras that can be seen by other spirits.

Similar to Bigfoot and mermaids, fairies can communicate both telepathically and with a verbal language. They have high, squeaky voices.

Both male and female fairies exist. And so does romance. However, since these heavenly creatures are spirits, there is no physical way they can create fairy children. This experience isn't needed for their purposes. Besides, they are very childlike themselves.

Although fairies enjoy living and playing outdoors, they come to Earth with an important function — to watch over and provide healing to the environment. They can be seen by animals as they go about their tasks and play. Because of their love for nature and healing energy, plants thrive around them. And although they wouldn't choose to reside in a dead patch of the woods, they will visit a place that needs a jump start on recovery. Healing the foliage of an area that has burned to the ground is a typical way they would do this.

Providing companionship, whether it's to spirits in Heaven or beings on planets, is another purpose of fairies. Traveling from place to place requires little effort. They are compassionate and friendly creatures, yet they're also feisty and often play tricks on humans. Sometimes, their pranks cause physical harm — but nothing serious. They have an intolerance for those who hurt the environment or other people. It's the unkind humans who are the targets of their vengeful behavior. For example, fairies might move a small object, like a rock, to cause someone to stub their toe. Or they might tinker with a vehicle to prevent it from starting. They also tap on windows, but most people brush this off as a bird or squirrel.

Fairies are able to accomplish these tasks — which seem unbelievable considering their size — because they are spirits and therefore have more access to energy from the other side than we do. And when they work as a group, they can easily manipulate objects much larger than themselves.

Sam enjoys spending time traveling around with fairies. She finds them funny, high-spirited, and adorable. "I just love them!"

Unicorns

Most of us presume unicorns are imaginary creatures, yet they've been around for centuries. They have never visited Earth or other planets, though.

These mystical animals were created by God as spirits whose main purpose is to bring more love and beauty to the other side. Their bodies are basically the same as those of horses except for the horns on their foreheads. And not all of them are white, as we picture them. They can be very colorful — pink, blue, green, yellow, and so on. They can also be the natural colors of earthly horses. And just as some spirits ride horses in the afterlife, they also ride unicorns.

If unicorns have never been to Earth, how did we end up picturing them? Since we know that spirits are constantly putting thoughts in our heads, it's logical that they would have sent images of these fun-loving creatures. We have also learned about unicorns from souls who have brought the memory of them from the other side when they incarnated into a life here.

Do Our Loved Ones in Spirit Want to Communicate with Us?

Our loved ones most definitely want to connect with us, and they try all the time. But if you're like me, you don't hear them speak aloud and you don't know which thoughts are yours and which are theirs. However, if you're thinking about something and a completely different thought — or a particularly profound thought — pops into your head, you might consider paying attention.

Most of us do not possess the abilities that gifted mediums do, but that doesn't mean we can't develop skills that will enhance our natural connection to the spirit world. Sam often suggests that I meditate, to give me practice in calming my mind so that I will be more receptive to hearing from her. Other than the handful of times that her words have come into my mind, I haven't advanced much in this pursuit. Unfortunately, whenever I relax enough to meditate, I fall asleep. But I do spend time every evening talking to Sam and listening for her in my head. The answers I get aren't always what I hope to hear, so maybe sometimes, it is her.

Sam has also suggested "automatic writing" as a way

to communicate with her: I write down a question I have for her (or any spirit), wait a minute or two, and then write whatever comes into my head. (Writing on paper is much more effective than typing on a computer or phone.) I find this approach helpful whenever I have a specific concern or issue. Either I will get an answer from Sam (or a guide), or I'll get my own thoughtfully considered resolution.

Our loved ones in spirit want to comfort us, but since many of us aren't sure — or aren't even aware — that we are hearing their messages, they give us signs to let us know they're with us.

How Do Spirits Send Us Signs?

There are several ways our departed loved ones reach out to us. They can send butterflies, birds, or other insects and animals (even skunks) to get our attention. They can come into a dream, alter the energy of electrical fixtures or battery-operated devices, produce a smell, manipulate computers and phones, and put songs on a music device or computer. Occasionally, some can move objects — such as feathers — and place them in unexpected places. I'm sure there are other types of signs, but these are the various ways Sam (and those that have assisted her) have either pranked or comforted me.

Not all spirits can do everything. They have different abilities at different levels. For example, Sam is good at interrupting the energy of a light fixture or a battery-operated alarm clock, but she cannot move something without the help of guides or angels. She can pop into my dreams but has done this only a few times. I dream about her often, yet only a handful of these are actual visits from her. It's easy for me to tell when they're truly her: the details are vivid, the message is beautiful, and I remember the dream as I would an event that happened while I was awake.

Sam can also play songs on my computer, phone, or TV (when I'm listening to Pandora) or manipulate the songs on my iPod. Once, with the help of an angel, she increased the volume of a song so much that I knew it was her. The song was Frank Sinatra's rendition of "No One Else Could Love You More." It was too loud to miss, which was her intention.

She even has the ability to make a small breeze on her own. But if she wants to cause a big wind, she must enlist the assistance of others.

Occasionally, a person is fortunate enough to see a loved one in spirit, but it's uncommon for souls to be seen in physical form here. Although every spirit has the potential to do this, usually it is an ability that must be worked on and developed. For some, it could take the equivalent of a thousand earthly years. And many don't have the desire or willingness to be seen, anyway. There are souls that can appear as a shadow or faint form but not as a complete figure. But whether a spirit can be seen, regardless of their form, also depends on the human's ability to see them.

Some people have felt the touch or hug of a spirit, but souls rarely touch us in a manner that we can perceive — Sam says this is because it would scare the hell out of most of us.

Millions of people believe they've received signs from the other side. I would estimate that more often than not, these are actual occurrences. Sam says that if a person truly feels like they are receiving a sign from someone, they probably are.

Why Do Souls Want to Come into a Life on Earth?

Again, not all souls will choose to incarnate into a life — any time or anywhere. But many do. Some souls might decide to experience life on a planet that's more intellectually advanced. Some might choose a planet where there's very little pain and illness. There are so many more planets than we're aware of, and each has its own characteristics. The souls that choose to come to Earth know that the struggles will be significant, as life is more difficult here than on most planets. It is these extreme challenges that provide more opportunities to learn and allow the soul to evolve more quickly. There are no struggles in Heaven; therefore, growth there requires more focus and will take longer.

The ultimate goal of those who come here is to be spiritually fulfilled enough that they don't feel the need to come back. Of course, any soul can stop incarnating into physical lives whenever they choose (or to never be born into a life). It's up to each soul to decide when they have reached a satisfying level of enlightenment. But even when they have reached that point, souls will continue to learn and grow on the other side.

The list of lessons planned for each life could be short or long. It all depends on how ambitious the soul is. Most who have experienced only a few lives will take on less. In general, the overall purpose of each life is to grow by completing objectives and to help others with theirs. But a select minority have a purpose that is broader. Many of these people will experience lives that include significant humanitarian efforts. Jesus is a great example. He was here to influence lives globally, for the greater good. There have also been horrible people whose souls sent them here with the intent of changing the world. Even if their actions resulted in the death of many, their lives could have been preplanned to affect and teach millions worldwide.

Lessons are divided into specific themes. Grief, trust, patience, compassion, independence, love, hate, greed, isolation, loneliness, rejection, abandonment, addiction, self-discipline, resourcefulness, envy, jealousy, anger, control, and self-righteousness are just some of the many areas souls could be working on.

Life on Earth isn't meant to be easy. If we didn't have struggles, it would be a waste of time to incarnate here. Whenever we're in pain, our departed loved ones and guides feel empathy for our suffering, but they don't think of it as unfortunate. They know it's part of why we came here — to learn from the challenges we planned. However, they feel delight when we find ways to minimize our anguish.

There are people who get stuck in the mindset of feeling victimized. And there are others who rise from their suffering — no matter how severe — by keeping a positive state of mind and doing whatever they can to improve their situation. Then there are those who are somewhere in the middle, fluctuating between optimism and negative thinking. It is natural to get upset and not always handle issues well; this is part of the human experience. Sometimes, we're meant to tackle things with blood, sweat, and tears.

During our life review, we won't feel disappointment if we didn't handle our lessons with grace. Instead, we will rejoice in the fact that we did learn them. No matter how messy our life experiences are, from the other side we'll view them with gratitude because we'll truly understand the purpose of them. And if we learn what we had planned, it will be a huge accomplishment that will be celebrated by many.

How Can We Make the Most of Our Time Here?

S ince evolving spiritually is the reason that most of us are here, we might as well endeavor to live life to the fullest. By doing this, we will have an abundance of opportunities to learn and grow.

Sam says self-awareness is the key to finding more happiness and joy. She implores us to focus on what we really want, and to not spend time or energy following the beliefs or ideas of others. We're here to have our own experiences.

However, supporting the needs and passions of others, as well as fulfilling our own, will enrich our lives. Some of our most important lessons will come from connecting with others. We can choose to give love or withhold it, but expressing kindness and compassion to our families, acquaintances, and even strangers will have a positive effect on everyone involved. Naturally, when we help others, there's a sense of fulfillment. Still, we need to allow others to help us, so that they have the opportunity to be more fulfilled as well.

In addition to self-awareness and connecting with others, we could get more out of life by striving to be more present — more in the moment. We can do this by expressing our love when we're with others and engaging our senses as much as possible: sight, sound, smell, taste, and touch. The more senses involved, the richer the experience.

Life will always have its ups and downs. If it didn't, we wouldn't have opportunities to evolve. Even though it has its difficulties, life doesn't have to be heavy. If we choose to see the lighter side of things, we will be able to deal with our struggles more easily. So, by following our desires and dreams, loving and supporting others, and living in the moment, we can experience our fullest lives.

Acknowledgments

Sam, I realize that I don't need to put into words my endless gratitude for your constant love and support — you already know what's in my heart. But I do want everyone to know how incredibly proud I am to have been your mother in this life. You were, and are, the sunshine of my life!

Jennifer Doran, your wonderful gifts of mediumship have provided me the opportunity to continue my deep connection with Sam and to learn about the workings of Heaven. Your abilities, compassion, and friendship have been a godsend.

To the family members who willingly listen to my out-of-this-world ramblings, I'm grateful that you haven't ignored me. You are one of the major reasons I continue to write.

Thank you to my editors, Teja and Rachel. Your caring spirit, open-mindedness, encouragement, and guidance have made a challenging task more enjoyable.

Christopher, I appreciate your endless patience and thoughtfulness. I can't imagine any publisher offering more support, sharing their knowledge, and giving their advice (personal or professional) when needed.

About the Author

Beverly Holliday, a former artist and teacher (math and art), recently discovered a new calling — writing about the incredible life that awaits us all after we leave this life. She lives with her husband in Tallahassee, Florida, in a cottage surrounded by an abundance of wildlife. Both she and her husband enjoy watching the comings and goings of deer, opossums, geese, raccoons, rabbits, and a big hawk named Melvin.

Following the unexpected loss of her daughter, Sam, she was inspired to find a way to communicate with her. After several years of recording conversations with Sam, Beverly wrote her first book, *Messages from Sam: A Daughter's Insights on Our Lives Here — And Her Life in Heaven*, a memoir that depicts Sam's time on Earth and many surprising details about the other side.

Beverly spends her time reading, walking, watching movies, beaching when she can, and writing about what she's learned from Sam, her father, and other loved ones.

Connect with her via email at messagesfromsam@yahoo.com.